THE

M   ENSON

ALSO BY MAY SWENSON

THE LOVE POEMS OF
MAY SWENSON

FOUR-WORD LINES

Your eyes are just
like bees, and I
feel like a flower.
Their brown power makes
a breeze go over
my skin. When your
lashes ride down and
rise like brown bees'
legs, your pronged gaze
makes my eyes gauze.
I wish we were
in some shade and
no swarm of other
eyes to know that
I'm a flower breathing
bare, laid open to
your bees' warm stare.
I'd let you wade
in me and seize
with your eager brown
bees' power a sweet
glistening at my core.

MORNINGS INNOCENT

I wear your smile upon my lips
arising on mornings innocent
Your laughter overflows my throat
Your skin is a fleece about me
With your princely walk I salute the sun
People say I am handsome

Arising on mornings innocent
birds make the sound of kisses
Leaves flicker light and dark like eyes

I melt beneath the magnet of your gaze
Your husky breath insinuates my ear
Alert and fresh as grass I wake

and rise on mornings innocent
The strands of the wrestler
run golden through my limbs
I cleave the air with insolent ease
With your princely walk I salute the sun
People say I am handsome

SWIMMERS

Tossed
by the muscular sea,
we are lost,
and glad to be lost
in troughs of rough

love. A bath in
laughter, our dive
into foam,
our upslide and float
on the surf of desire.

But sucked to the root
of the water-mountain —
immense —
about to tip upon us
the terror of total

delight —
we are towed,
helpless in its
swell, by hooks
of our hair;

then dangled, let go,
made to race —
as the wrestling chest
of the sea, itself
tangled, tumbles

in its own embrace.
Our limbs like eels
are water-boned,
our faces lost
to difference and

contour, as the lapping
crests.
They cease
their charge,
and rock us

in repeating hammocks
of the releasing
tide —
until supine we glide,
on cool green

smiles
of an exhaling
gladiator,
to the shore
of sleep.

EARLY MORNING: CAPE COD

We wake to double blue:
an ocean without sail,
sky without a clue
of white.
Morning is a veil
sewn of only two
threads, one pale,
one bright.

We bathe as if in ink,
but peacock-eyed and clear;
a roof of periwink
goes steep
into a bell of air
vacant to the brink.
Far as we can peer
is deep

royal blue and shy
iris, queen and king
colors of low
and high.
Then dips
a sickle wing,
we hear a hinged cry:
taut as from a sling

downwhips
a taunting gull.
And now across our gaze
a snowy hull
appears;
triangles
along its stays
break out to windpulls.

With creaking shears
the bright
gulls cut the veil
in two,
and many a clue
on scalloped sail
dots with white
our double blue.

We go to gather berries of rain
(sharp to the eye as ripe to the tongue)
that cluster the woods and, low down
between rough-furrowed pine
trunks, melons of sunlight. Morning, young,
carries a harvest in its horn:
colors, shapes, odors, tones
(various as senses are keen).
High in a grape-transparent fan
of boughs are cones
of crystal that were wooden brown.

Two by two, into our ears
are fed sweet pips from a phoebe's throat,
and buzzy notes from a warbler pair,
nuts chuckled from the score
of the thrasher. Gauzing afloat,
a giant moth comes to the choir,
and hums while he sips
from spangles of fern. Insects whir
like wheat in a circular
bin of light; we hear skip
the husking chipmunks in their lair.

Goblin pears, or apples, or quaint
eggs, the mushrooms
litter the forest loft
on pungent mats, in shade still wet,
the gray of gunny in the gloom —
in sun, bright sawdust.
Here's a crop for the nose:
(relish to sight as motley to scent):
fume of cobwebbed stumps, musky roots,
resin-tincture, bark-balm, dayspring moss
in stars new-pricked (vivid as soft).

Day heats and mellows. Those winking seeds —
or berries — spill from their pods; the path's dry
from noon wood to meadow. A speckled
butterfly on top of a weed is a red
and yellow bloom: if that two-ply
petal could be touched,
or the violet wing of the mountain!
Both out of reach — too wary,
or too far to stroke, unless with the eye.
But in green silk of the rye
grain our whole bodies are cuddled.

In the sun's heart we are ripe
as fruits ourselves, enjoyed
by lips of wind our burnished slopes.
All round us dark, rapt
bumble-eyes of susans are deployed
as if to suck our honey-hides. Ants nip,
tasting us all over
with tickling pincers. We are a landscape
to daddy-long-legs, whose ovoid
hub on stilts climbs us like a lover,
trying our dazzle, our warm sap.

EACH DAY OF SUMMER

In the unassembled puzzle of the city
a lava forest ragged crags of roofs
to a ledge hung in rare green
and a narrow garden
in immutable rock a fissure
of living grass
the sun came like a king
each day of summer
with great golden hands
caressed our skin to jasper

Miraculous as if a mounted knight
crowned caparisoned crossed a soot-grim moat
to a round tower ribbon-tipped
each day of summer
love came bearing love
a chalice of light
We bathed in love and drank it
Then our flesh
seemed like the leaves
enameled bright forever

Now the roofs are white with winter's order
the city's million gashes bandaged clean
earth and sinuous tree
stern brick and cobble
by ethereal snow composed to unity
The ledge where the sun
a coat of mail lay on us
now a coffer loaded with pearls of frost
the opulent plume in warm blue
that waved above us
now stark as ivory canopied in gray

But the honey in our veins burned deep
We are stored with sweetness
Our breasts are golden hives
In interior bone
the scepter's knob hoards ruby like a coal
In the eternal sky of mind
each day of summer
paints a lozenge in the prism of our love

A loaf of time
round and thick
So many layers
ledges to climb
to lie on our
bellies lolling
licking our lips
The long gaze a
gull falling
down the cliff's
table   to coast
the constant
waves   The reach-
ing wave-tongues
lick the table
But slowly grayly
slow as the ocean
is gray beyond
the green   slow
as the sky is high
and out of sight
higher than blue
is white   Around
the table's wheel
unbounded   for
each a meal the
centered mound to
be divided   A
wedge for each
and leisure on
each ledge   The
round loaf thick
we lick our lips
Our eyes gull

down the layered
cliff and ride
the reaching waves
that lick but   slowly
the table's
edge   Then slowly
our loaf   Slowly
our ledge

IN THE YARD

Dogwood's s n o w. Its ground's air.
R e d h e a d e d's riddling the phone pole.

Fat-tailed she-dog grinning's
t h r a s h e r - r e d.

It's the oriole there by the feeder
c h e d d a r under b l a c k bold head.

Neighbor doing yardwork's getting r e d.
Lifts tiles to a barrow.

L.I.R.R.'s four cars rollskate by
w h i t e potato blooms farside the field.

That square's our bedroom window.
You're not there. You're away

looking for nails or such
to put up a mirror frame the Adam

and Eve bright hair held back by a
r o b i n's - e g g - b l u e band.

Or you're at the body shop about
the broken bumper.

C a b b a g e b u t t e r f l y's found
h o n e y he thinks on r i n g

g l i n t s on my hand. I wait
for the r i n g n e c k who

noseblows twice parades his mate. She's g r a y.
Until comes the B l u e Bug crunching driveway.

You're back barefoot brought some fruit.
Split me a n a p p l e. We'll get r e d

w h i t e halves each our
juice on the Indian spread.

A COUPLE

A bee
rolls
in the yellow
rose.
Does she
invite his hairy
rub?

He scrubs
himself
in her creamy
folds;
a bullet, soft, imposes
her spiral and, spinning, burrows
to her dewy
shadows.

The gold
grooves almost
match
the yellow
bowl.
Does his touch
please
or scratch?

When he's
done
his honey-
thieving
at her matrix,
whirs free
leaving,
she

closes,
still
tall, chill,
unrumpled on her stem.

CAFÉ TABLEAU

Hand of the copper boy
pours tea   deft wrist square fist
salmon-satin-lined

Dark-muscled dancers among porcelain
twined   his fingers and long thumb

He stands dumb in crisp white coat
his blood in heavy neck-vein
eloquent   its flood plunges
to each purple nail   emanates
male electrons

His pupils conscienceless as midnight skies
between the moon-whites of his eyes   avoid
tea-sipper's naked shoulder
diamond-cold her throat

That she is female his broad nostrils
have denied   like figs dried when green
her breasts shrivel in the refusal
of his stare

His thigh athletic slender   retreats
behind her chair   in his hips
nothing tender   ancestral savagery
has left him lion-clean

Furtive beneath mental hedges
she sees   feels his bare wrist square fist
her boneless hand creeps up the crisp sleeve
higher   she squeals and finds the nipples
of his hairless chest

The copper boy's white coat
becomes a loincloth she unwinds   he wades
into the pool of her stagnant desire

OUR FORWARD SHADOWS

all we see as yet
slant tall
and timid
on the floor

the stage is set
each waits
in the long-lit door

a bell in the wings
far in the painted forest
rings announcing delight

ourselves
still out of sight
our shadows listen

the cue
summons the dance
of me and you

advance
where our shadows meet
already loved

invade the room
with the scent
of thunder in the blood

move on the colored flood
naked
needing no costume

we are dressed
each in the other's kisses

our shadows reach
to teach us our parts

the enchanted prelude starts

ORGANS

hidden in the hair
the spiral Ear
waits to Suck sound

and sly beneath its
ledge the Eye to Spear
the fish of light

the Mouth's a hole
and yet a Cry for
love for loot

with every stolen
breath the Snoot
Supposes roses

nose tongue fishing
eye's Crouched
in the same hutch

nibbling lips and
funnel's there
in the legs' lair
carnivora of Touch

FACING

1

You I love
you are that light
by which I am discovered.
In anonymous night
by your eye am I born.
And I know
that by your body I glow,
and by your face
I make my circle.
It is your heat
fires me
that my skin is sweet
my veins race
my bones are radiant.

You are that central One
by which I am balanced.
By your power it is done
that in the sky of being
my path is thrown.
And I glide in your sling
and cannot fall into darkness.
For by the magnet
of your body
charged with love
do I move.

2

As you are sun to me
O I am moon to you.
And give you substance
by my sight
and motion and radiance.
You are an ocean
shaped by my gaze.
My pulsing rays
draw you naked
from the spell of night.
By my pull
are you waked
to know that you are beautiful.

I rake up your steep
luster and your passion;
by my sorcery your wealth is sown
to you on your own breast,
your purples changed to opals.

So with love's light
I sculpture you
and in my constant mirror keep
your portrait
that you may adore
yourself as I do.

Two white whales have been installed at
the Waldorf. They are tumbling slowly
above the tables, butting the chandeliers,
submerging, and taking soft bites
out of the red-vested waiters in the
Peacock Room. They are poking *fleur-de-lys*
tails into the long pockets on the
waiters' thighs. They are stealing
breakfast strawberries from two eccentric
guests — one, skunk-cabbage green with
dark peepers — the other, wild rose and
milkweed, barelegged, in Lafayette loafers.
When the two guests enter the elevator,
the whales ascend, bouncing, through all
the ceilings, to the sixth floor. They
get between the sheets. There they turn
candy-pink, with sky-colored eyes, and
silver bubbles start to rise from velvet
navels on the tops of their heads.
Later, a pale blue VW, running on poetry,
weaves down Park Avenue, past yellow
sprouts of forsythia, which, due to dog-do
and dew, are doing nicely. The two
white whales have the blue car in tow
on a swaying chain of bubbles. They are
rising toward the heliport on the Pan Am
roof. There they go, dirigible and slow,
hide-swiping each other, lily tails flipping,
their square velvet snouts stitched with
snug smiles. It is April. "There's
a kind of hush all over the world."

TO F.

The el ploughs down the morning
The newsboys stand in wait
Sunlight lashes the cobbles
We reach the crosstown gate

Your bus will stop at Christopher
Mine at Abingdon Square
Your hand . . . "Good luck" and mine . . . "So long"
The taxi trumpets blare

The green light turns, a whistle blows
Our steps divide the space
Between our day-long destinies
But still I see your face

Whirling through the crowded hours
Down the afternoon
Lurking in my thoughts, your smile
Pricks me like a tune

The acrobat astride his swing in space
the pole rolled under his instep
catches the pits of his knees
is lipped by his triangled groin
fits the fold of his hard-carved buttocks

Long-thighed tight-hipped he drops
head-down and writhes erect
glazed smooth by speed a twirled top
sits immobile in the void

Gravity outwhipped squeezed like dough
is kneaded to his own design
a balance-egg at the plexus of his bowels
counteracting vertigo

Empty of fear and therefore without weight
he walks a wedge of steeper air
indifferent to the enormous stare
of onlookers in rims of awe below

Drums are solid blocks beneath him
Strong brass horn-tones prolong him
on glittering stilts

Self-hurled he swims the color-stippled height
where nothing but whisks of light
can reach him

At night he is my lover

AUGUST NIGHT

Shadow like a liquid lies
   in your body's hollows
In your eyes garnet stars
   shift their facets with your breath
The August night is Nubian
   something green mixed with the dark
a powder for your skin that tints
   the implications of your bones
with copper light
   an aura round your knees your navel
a little pool with pulsing tide

Is there beauty deeper than your cool
   form drawn by the occult stylus
of this night
   slanting to autumn
the long dawn soon bringing wrappings
   for your breast?
Has any other watchman stiller stayed
   to the smiting of this gong
half in glory half afraid to look
   at what obscure in light
is now explained by shade?

FIREFLIES

Fireflies throw
love winks
to their kind
on the dark, glow
without heat,

their day bodies
common beetles.
In a planetarium
of the mind
sparks lit

when logic has gone
down
faint in the dawn
of intellect.
Instinct

makes luminous
the insect.
Idea's anonymous
ordinary mark,
that cryptic

in daylight crept,
can rise an asterisk
astonishing others out.
If the secret
of the dark

be kept,
an eagerness
in smallest, fiercest
hints
can scintillate.

IN LOVE MADE VISIBLE

In love are we made visible
As in a magic bath
are unpeeled
to the sharp pit
so long concealed

With love's alertness
we recognize
the soundless whimper
of the soul
behind the eyes
A shaft opens
and the timid thing
at last leaps to surface
with full-spread wing

The fingertips of love discover
more than the body's smoothness
They uncover a hidden conduit
for the transfusion
of empathies that circumvent
the mind's intrusion

In love are we set free
Objective bone
and flesh no longer insulate us
to ourselves alone
We are released
and flow into each other's cup
Our two frail vials pierced
drink each other up

YEAR OF THE DOUBLE SPRING

Passing a lank boy, bangs to the eyebrows,
licking a Snow Flake cone, and cones on the tulip tree
   up stiff, honeysuckle tubelets weighting a vine,
and passing *Irene Gay — Realtor, The Black Whale, Rexall,*
   and others — (Irene, don't sue me, it's just your sign
I need in the scene) —
   remembering lilac a month back, a different faded shade,
buying a paper with the tide table instead of the twister
   forecast on page three,
then walking home from the village, beneath the viaduct,
   I find Midwest echoes answering echoes
that another, yet the same train, wakes here out East.
   I'm thinking of how I leaned on you, you leaning
in the stone underpass striped with shadows of tracks
   and ties, and I said, "Give me a kiss, A.D.,
even if you are tranquilized," and I'm thinking
   of the Day of the Kingfisher, the Indigo Day of the Bunting,
of the Catfish Night I locked the keys in the car
   and you tried to jimmy in, but couldn't, with a clothes hanger.
The night of the juke at Al's — *When Something's Wrong*
   With My Baby — you pretended to flake out on the bench,
and I poured icy Scotch into the thimble of your belly,
   lifting the T-shirt. Another night you threw up
in a Negro's shoe. It's Accabonac now instead of
   Tippecanoe. I'm remembering how we used to drive
to *The Custard* "to check out the teenage boxes."
   I liked the ones around the Hondas, who
from a surly distance, from under the hair in their eyes,
   cruised the girls in flowered shorts.
One day back there, licking cones, we looked in
   on a lioness lying with her turd behind the gritty window
of a little zoo. I liked it there. I'd like it
   anywhere with you.
Here there are gorgeous pheasants, no hogs, blond horses,

and Alec Guinness seen at *The Maidstone* Memorial Eve —
and also better dumps. You scavenged my plywood desk top,
   a narrow paint-flecked old door, and the broad white
wicker I'm sitting in now.
   While you're at the dump hunting for more —
maybe a double spring good as that single you climbed to
   last night (and last year) — I sit in front of a house,
remembering a house back there, thinking of a house —
   where? when? — by spring next year?
I notice the immature oak leaves, vivid as redbud almost,
   and shaped like the spoor of the weasel we saw
once by the Wabash.
   Instead of "to the *Readmore*" riffling *Playboy*, I found
you yesterday in that Newtown Lane newspaper store
   I don't yet know the name of. Stay with me, A.D.,
don't blow. Scout out that bed. Go find tennis
   instead of squash mates, surfboarders, volleyball
boys to play with. I know you will, before long —
   maybe among the lifeguards — big, cool-coned,
straight-hipped, stander-on-one-finger, strong.

Unloosed, unharnessed, turned back to the wild by love,
the ring you cantered round with forelock curled,
the geometric music of this world
dissolved and, in its place,
alien as snow to tropic tigers, amphitheatric space,
you will know the desert's freedom, wind and sun
rough-currying your mane, the plenitude
of strong caresses on your body nude.

Released to run from me. Then will I stand
alone in the hoof-torn ring,
lax in my hand
as wine leaked out the thin whip of my will,
and gone the lightning-string
between your eye and mine.

Our discipline was mutual and the art
that spun our dual beauty. While you wheeled
in flawless stride apart,
I, in glittering boots to the fulcrum heeled,
need hardly signal: your prideful head
plunged to the goad of love-looks sharper than ice.

I gloated on the palomino of your flanks, the nice
sprightliness of pace,
your posture like Apollo's steed. I stood my place
as in a chariot,
held the thong of studded light, the lariat
that made you halt, or longer leap, or faster.
But you have bridled me, bright master.

On wild, untrampled slopes you will be monarch soon,
and I the mount that carries you to those high

prairies steeped in noon.
In the arena where your passion will be spent
in loops of speed, sky's indigo unbounded
by the trainer's tent,
instead of oboes, thunder's riddle,
rain for the racing fifes, I will be absent.

When orchestras of air shall vault you
to such freedom, joy and power,
I will cut the whip that sent you there, will put
away the broken ring, and shut
the school of my desire.

POET TO TIGER

The Hair

You went downstairs
saw a hair in the sink
and squeezed my toothpaste by the neck.
You roared. My ribs are sore.
This morning even my pencil's got your toothmarks.
Big Cat Eye cocked on me you see bird bones.
Snuggled in the rug of your belly
your breath so warm
I smell delicious fear.
Come breathe on me rough pard
put soft paws here.

The Salt

You don't put salt on anything
so I'm eating without.
Honey on the eggs is all right
mustard on the toast.
I'm not complaining I'm saying I'm
living with *you.*
You like your meat raw
don't care if it's cold.
Your stomach must have tastebuds
you swallow so fast.
Night falls early. It's foggy. Just now

I found another of your bite marks in the cheese.
I'm hungry. Please
come bounding home
I'll hand you the wine to open
with your teeth.
Scorch me a steak unsalted
boil my coffee twice

say the blessing to a jingle on the blue TV.
Under the lap robe on our chilly couch
look behind my ears "for welps"
and hug me.

The Sand

You're right I brought a grain
or two of sand
into bed I guess in my socks.
But it was you pushed them off
along with everything else.

Asleep you flip
over roll
everything under
you and off
me. I'm always grabbing
for my share of the sheets.

Or else you wake me every hour with sudden
growled I-love-yous
trapping my face between those plushy
shoulders. All my float-dreams turn spins
and never finish. I'm thinner
now. My watch keeps running fast.
But best is when we're riding pillion
my hips within your lap. You let me steer.
Your hand and arm go clear
around my ribs your moist
dream teeth fastened on my nape.

A grain of sand in the bed upsets you or
a hair on the floor.
But you'll get

33

in slick and wet from the shower if I let
you. Or with your wool cap
and skiing jacket on
if it's cold.
Tiger don't scold me
don't make me comb my hair outdoors.

Cuff me careful. Lick don't
crunch. Make last what's yours.

The Dream

You get into the tub holding *The Naked Ape*
in your teeth. You wet that blond
three-cornered pelt lie back wide
chest afloat. You're reading
in the rising steam and I'm
drinking coffee from your tiger cup.
You say you dreamed
I had your baby book
and it was pink and blue.
I pointed to a page and there
was your face with a cub grin.

You put your paws in your armpits
make a tiger-moo.
Then you say: "Come here
Poet and take
this hair
off me." I do.
It's one of mine. I carefully
kill it and carry
it outside. And stamp on it
and bury it.

In the begonia bed.
And then take off my shoes
not to bring a grain
of sand in to get
into our bed.
I'm going to
do the cooking
now instead
of you.
And sneak some salt in
when you're not looking.

A HISTORY OF LOVE

Other than self
O inconceivable
How touched how kissed?
There was a lodestone
made the stars rush down
like pins that fastened us together
under the same dark cloak
We were stroked
by some magician's fur

Each became a doll
Our pure amazement
bestowed us perfect gifts
Our cravings were surpassed
by the porcelain eyes
alluring lips caressable hair
Undressed we handled ivory idols

Summer winter fall and still delighted
unmarred in the dangerous game of change
Replaced by the wonder of the found
the so long kept
The dear endurable surprised us more
than the ecstasies of ritual spring
Like Nature her transfers we adored our everydays
the never knowing what
next the sprites within us would disclose

At last acquainted smoothed by contiguity
sharpened each by opposite tempers we divined
about our nacreous effigies outlined
the soft and mortal other
Under the body's plush a density
awkward ambiguous as bone
Real as our own

O other than self
and O believable
The dream tent fallen
daylight come
we wake to a nakedness so actual
our magnet a common innocent stone

Else than beauty
else than passion then?
Their amalgam mingled mounted up to this
How sweet the plain
how warm the true
We by this mystery charmed anew
begin again to love

ANOTHER ANIMAL

Another animal imagine moving
  in his rippling hide
    down the track of the centaur
      Robust inside him his heart siphons unction to his muscles
        proving
          this columnar landscape lives
            Last night's dream
              flinches at the mind's lattice
              transformed into a seam of sunlight on his trunk
            that like a tree
          shimmers in ribbons of shadow
        His mystery the invert cloud engulfs me with the grass

    Imagine another moving
  even as I pass
among the trees that need not shift their feet
  to pierce the sky's academy
    and let go their leaves
      let go
        their leaves
          bright desperate as cries
            and do not cry
              Even as I he breathes
                and shall be breathless
              for the mind-connected pulse
            heaves hurries halts for but two reasons
          Loveless then deathless
        but if loved
      surrendered to the season's summit
    the ice-hood the volcano's hiccough
  the empty-orbed zero of eclipse

The lean track dips together where our feet have pounced
   The rugs the pine boughs gave us glisten clean
      We meet like two whelps at their mother's dugs
         Does the earth trounced here recall
            the hipmarks of another fall
               when dappled animals with hooves and human knees
                  coupled in the face of the convulsive spurning
                     of other cities and societies?

         We are wizards mete for burning
         and rush forward to our fate
         neighing as when centaurs mate

      Unable to imagine until late
   in the September wood
that another stood out of God's pocket
   straddled between beast and human
      now each the other's first stern teacher
         learns the A and B against the bitten lips
            Our coiled tongues strike the first word
            Turned heels our star-crossed hands
               kick the mind to its ditch in leaf-mold
                  Open to joy to punishment in equal part
                     closed to the next mutation
                        we lie locked at the forking of the heart

SECURE

Let us deceive ourselves a little
while   Let us pretend that air
is earth   and falling lie resting
within each other's gaze   Let us

deny that flame consumes   that
fruit ripens   that the wave must
break   Let us forget the circle's
fixed beginning marks to the
instant its ordained end   Let us

lean upon the moment and expect
time to enfold us   space sustain
our weight   Let us be still   and
falling lie face to face and drink
each other's breath   Be still
Let us be still   We lie secure

within the careful mind of death

YOU ARE

you are my mirror
in your eye's well I float
my reality proven
                I dwell
                in you
                and so
                I know
                I am

no one
can be sure
by himself
of his own being
                     and the world's seeing
                  the fleeting mirrors of others' eyes
                  cloudy abstracted remote
                  or too bright convex false directly smiling
                  or crepuscular under their lids
                  crawling the ground like snails
                  or narrowed
                  nervously hooked to the distance
                     is suspect
do I live
does the world live
do I live in it
or does it live in me?
                  because you believe I exist I exist
                  I exist in your verdant garden
                     you have planted me
                     I am glad to grow
I dream of your hands by day
all day I dream of evening
when you will open the gate
come out of the noisy world
to tend me

to pour at my roots
the clear the flashing water
of your love
and exclaim over my new leaf
and stroke it with a broad finger
as if a god surprised fondled his first earth-sprig

once I thought
to seek the limits
of all being
I believed
in my own eyes' seeing
then
to find pattern purpose aim
thus forget death
or forgive it
then I thought
to plumb the heart of death
to cicatrize that spot
and plot abolishment
so that pattern shape and purpose
would not gall me
I would be its part forever
content in never falling
from its web

now I know
beginning and end
are one
and slay each other
but their offspring is what *is*
not was or will be

am I? yes
and never was
until you made me
crying there you are!
and I unfurled in your rich soil
I am the genie
in your eye's well
crouching there
so that you must take me with you everywhere
an underwater plant in a secret cylinder
                    you the vial
                    and I the vine
                    and I twining inside you

and you glad
to hold me
floating there
                    for if I live in you
                    you live holding me
                    enfolding me you *are*
it is proven and the universe exists!
                    one reflects the other
                    man mirrors god
                    image in eye affirms its sight
                    green stem in earth attests
                    its right to spin
                    in palpable roundness

is this then
what is meant
that god is love
and is that all?

how simple and how sure
at the very hub of hazard
so seeming fearful fragile insecure
two threads
in the web of chaos
lashed by the dark daemonic wind
crossed upon each other
therefore fixed and still
axial in the bursting void
are perpetual each according to the other
I am
then I am a garden too
and tend you

              my eye is a mirror
              in which you float
              a well where you dwell smiling
I the vial
hold you
a vine a twining genie
I enfold you
and secrete the liquid
of your being
in that I love you
and you live *in* me

THE TIGER'S GHOST

The tiger
and the tiger's passion
haunt this cell
in their own fashion

These cool walls
this empty place
remember well
the tiger's face
remember well
the tiger's yawn
as candle-eyed
he grinned upon
a stain of moonlight
on the floor
cleft by bars

The tiger's roar
consumed this silence
roused this stone
to raucous echo

O alone
the tiger stretched
on velvet flank
lapped by night

This room is rank
with carnal rage
and jungle smell
The tiger's ghost
lurks in this cell

I had a dream in which I had a
dream,
and in my dream I told you,
"Listen, I will tell you my
dream." And I began to tell you. And
you told me, "I haven't time to listen while you tell your
dream."

Then in my dream I
dreamed I began to
forget my
dream.
And I forgot my
dream.
And I began to tell you, "Listen, I have
forgot my
dream."
And now I tell you: "Listen while I tell you my
dream, a
dream
in which I dreamed I
forgot my
dream,"
and I begin to tell you: "In my dream you told me, 'I haven't time to
listen.' "

And you tell me: "You dreamed I wouldn't
listen to a
dream that you
forgot?
I haven't time to listen to
forgotten
dreams."

        "But I haven't forgot I
                  dreamed," I tell you,
           "a dream in which I told you,
                  'Listen, I have
                  forgot,' and you told me, 'I haven't time.' "
"I haven't time," you tell me.

        And now I begin to forget that I
                  forgot what I began to tell you in my
                  dream.
        And I tell you, "Listen,
                  listen, I begin to
                  forget."

WILD WATER

Insidious cruelty is this
that will allow the heart
a scent of wild water
in the arid land —
that holds out the cup
but to withdraw the hand.

Then says to the heart: Be glad
that you have beheld the font
where lies requitement,
and identified your thirst.
Now, heart, take up your desert;
this spring is cursed.

STONE OR FLAME

Shall we pray to be delivered
from the crying of the flesh
Shall we live like the lizard
in the frost of denial

Or shall we offer the nerve-buds
of our bodies
to be nourished (or consumed)
in the sun of love

Shall we wrap ourselves rigid
against desire's contagion
in sarcophagi of safety
insulate ourselves
from both fire and ice

And will the vessel of the heart
stay warm
if our veins be drained of passion
Will the spirit rise virile
from the crematory ash

Shall we borrow
from the stone
relentless peace
or from the flame
exquisite suicide?

THE KEY TO EVERYTHING

Is there anything I can do
or has everything been done
or do
you prefer somebody else to do
it or don't
you trust me to do
it right or is it hopeless and no one can do
a thing or do
you suppose I don't
really want to do
it and am just saying that or don't
you hear me at all or what?

You're
waiting for
the right person the doctor or
the nurse the father or
the mother or
the person with the name you keep
mumbling in your sleep
that no one ever heard of there's no one
named that really
except yourself maybe

If I knew what your name was I'd
prove it's your
own name spelled backwards or
twisted in some way the one you
keep mumbling but you
won't tell me your
name or
don't you know it
yourself that's it
of course you've

forgotten or
never quite knew it or
weren't willing to believe it

Then there *is* something I
can do I
can find your name for you
that's the key to everything once you'd
repeat it clearly you'd
come awake you'd
get up and walk knowing where you're
going where you
came from

And you'd
love me
after that or would you
hate me?
no once you'd
get there you'd
remember and love me
of course I'd
be gone by then I'd
be far away

THE WILLETS

One stood still, looking stupid. The other,
beak open, streaming a thin sound,
held wings out, took sideways steps,
stamping the salt marsh. It looked threatening.
The other still stood wooden, a decoy.

He stamp-danced closer, his wings arose,
their hinges straightened,
from the wedge-wide beak the thin sound
streaming agony-high —
in fear she wouldn't stand? She stood.

Her back to him pretended —
was it welcome, or only dazed
admission of their fate?
Lifting, he streamed a warning
from his beak, and lit

upon her, trod upon her
back, both careful feet.
The wings held off his weight.
His tail pressed down, slipped off. She
animated. And both went back to fishing.

HOLDING THE TOWEL

You swam out
through the boats
your head an orange

buoy sun-daubed
bobbing. My squint
lost you to nibbling

waves. I looked
for a mast to tilt
to glint with your splash

but couldn't see
past the huddled boats.
I found round heads sun-red

dipping rising tipping.
They were tethered
floats. When you dove

from the stovepipe
buoy in the far
furrow of the channel

I was still
scanning the nearby
nowhere-going boats.

THE INDIVISIBLE INCOMPATIBLES

They are like flame and ice
the elemental You and Me
Will nothing then suffice
but they shall extinguished be?

I am locked in glacial pride
You burn with impetuous scorn
My prison is silence
Your arena is wrath
They are opposed as night and morn

If this is so how can it be
we sought each other long ago
and crept together hungrily?

You are quenched in my cold heart
as I dissolve in your core of fire
Then why do we crave each other's touch
magnetized by one desire?

When one forged his armor so
bright as ice and cold as slate
did he divine a spear so swift
and savage as to penetrate?

When one wrapped himself in flame
and emerged a glowing tool
did he dream of substances
irresistible and cool?

Yes
but in fusion
such raw alloys
instantly each the other destroys

BIRTHDAY BUSH

Our bush bloomed, soon dropped
its fuchsia chalices. Rags
on the ground that were luscious
cups and trumpets, promises and brags.

A sprinkle of dark dots showed entry
into each silk cone. Down among
crisp pistils thirsty bumblebees
probed. Buds flared in a bunch

from tender stems. Sudden
vivid big bouquets
appeared just before our birthdays!
A galaxy our burning bush,

blissful explosion. Brief
effusion. Brief as these
words. I sweep away a trash
of crimson petals.

LITTLE LION FACE

Little lion face
I stooped to pick
among the mass of thick
succulent blooms, the twice

streaked flanges of your silk
sunwheel relaxed in wide
dilation, I brought inside,
placed in a vase. Milk

of your shaggy stem
sticky on my fingers, and
your barbs hooked to my hand,
sudden stings from them

were sweet. Now I'm bold
to touch your swollen neck,
put careful lips to slick
petals, snuff up gold

pollen in your navel cup.
Still fresh before night
I leave you, dawn's appetite
to renew our glide and suck.

An hour ahead of sun
I come to find you. You're
twisted shut as a burr,
neck drooped unconscious,

an inert, limp bundle,
a furled cocoon, your
sun-streaked aureole
eclipsed and dun.

Strange feral flower asleep
with flame-ruff wilted,
all magic halted,
a drink I pour, steep

in the glass for your
undulant stem to suck.
Oh, lift your young neck,
open and expand to your

lover, hot light.
Gold corona, widen to sky.
I hold you lion in my eye
sunup until night.

MORTAL SURGE

We are eager
We pant
We whine like whips cutting the air
The frothing sea
the roaring furnace
the jeweled eyes of animals call to us
and we stand frozen
moving neither forward nor back

In the breathless wedge between night and dawn
when the rill of blood pauses at the sluice of the heart
either to advance or retreat
the stars stare at us face to face
penetrating even the disguise of our nakedness
daring us to make the upward leap
effortless as falling
if only we relax the bowstring of our will

We seek the slippery flesh of other men
expecting to be comforted
or to be punished
or to be delighted beyond imagined delights
to be made clean
or to be baptized in the cool font of evil

We believe in the meeting of lips
in the converging of glances
that a talisman is given
that we shall arise anew
be healed and made whole
or be torn at last from our terrible womb-twin
our very self

We are loved in the image of the dead
We love in the image of the never-born
We shudder to beget with child

We shudder not to beget with child
We scream in the doorway of our beginning
We weep at the exit gate

We are alone and never alone
bound and never secured
let go and never freed
We would dance and are hurled
would build and are consumed
We are dragged backward by the past
jerked forward by the future

Our earth a bloody clot of the sun's cataclysm
sun a severed limb of a shattered universe
In fission
explosion
In separation
congealment

ALL THAT TIME

I saw two trees embracing.
One leaned on the other
as if to throw her down.
But she was the upright one.
Since their twin youth, maybe she
had been pulling him toward her
all that time,

and finally almost uprooted him.
He was the thin, dry, insecure one,
the most wind-warped, you could see.
And where their tops tangled
it looked like he was crying
on her shoulder.
On the other hand, maybe he

had been trying to weaken her,
break her, or at least
make her bend
over backwards for him
just a little bit.
And all that time
she was standing up to him

the best she could.
She was the most stubborn,
the straightest one, that's a fact.
But he had been willing
to change himself —
even if it was for the worse —
all that time.

At the top they looked like one
tree, where they were embracing.
It was plain they'd be
always together.
Too late now to part.
When the wind blew, you could hear
them rubbing on each other.

DREAMS AND ASHES

Only on the anvil's edge
where the blue fire flashes
will my lead love turn to gold
The rest is dreams and ashes

Only in sleep or solitude
where fancy's fountain plashes
will my dead love rise to swim
The rest is dreams and ashes

Only on the unmarked page
wherever the bold mind dashes
will my fled love follow me
The rest is dreams and ashes

UNTITLED

I   will   be   earth   you   be   the   flower
You   have   found   my   root   you   are   the   rain
I   will   be   boat   and   you   the   rower
You   rock   you   toss   me   you   are   the   sea
How   be   steady   earth   that's   now   a   flood
The   root's   the   oar's   afloat   where's   blown   our   bud
We   will   be   desert   pure   salt   the   seed
Burn   radiant   sex   born   scorpion   need

SATANIC FORM

Numerals forkmarks of Satan
Triangles circles squares
hieroglyphs of death
Things invented
abortions smelling of the forge
licked to gruesome smoothness by the lathe
Things metallic or glass
frozen twisted flattened
stretched to agonized bubbles
Bricks beams receptacles vehicles
forced through fire hatched to unwilling form
O blasphemies
Time caught in a metal box
Incongruous the rigid clucking tongue
the needled hands the 12-eyed face
against the open window past which drops the night
like a dark lake on end or flowing hair
Night unanimous over all the city
The knuckled fist of the heart opening and closing
Flower and stone not cursed with symmetry
Cloud and shadow not doomed to shape and fixity
The intricate body of man without rivet or nail
or the terrible skirl of the screw
O these are blessed
Satanic form geometry of death
The lariat around the neck of space
The particles of chaos in the clock
The bottle of the yellow liquor light
that circumvents the sifting down of night
O love the juice in the green stem growing
you cannot synthesize
It corrodes in phials and beakers
evaporates in the hot breath of industry
escapes to the air and the dew
returns to the root of the unborn flower
O Satan cheated of your power

It is the last night of the world.
I am allowed once more to show my love.
I place a jewel on a cushion.
I make a juggler's trick.
I become a graceful beast to play with you.

See here something precious, something dazzling:
A garden to be your home,
vast and with every fruit.
The air of mountains for your garment.
The sun to be your servant.
A magic water for you to bathe in
and step forth immortal.

But it is the last night of the world,
and time itself is dying.
Tomorrow my love, locked in the box of my body,
will be shipped away.

THE SHAPE OF DEATH

What does love look like? We know
the shape of death. Death is a cloud
immense and awesome. At first a lid
is lifted from the eye of light:
There is a clap of sound, a white blossom

belches from the jaw of fright,
a pillared cloud churns from white to gray
like a monstrous brain that bursts and burns,
then turns sickly black, spilling away,
filling the whole sky with ashes of dread;

thickly it wraps, between the clean sea
and the moon, the earth's green head.
Trapped in its cocoon, its choking breath,
we know the shape of death:
Death is a cloud.

What does love look like?
Is it a particle, a star —
invisible entirely, beyond the microscope and Palomar?
A dimension unimagined, past the length of hope?
Is it a climate far and fair that we shall never dare

discover? What is its color, and its alchemy?
Is it a jewel in the earth — can it be dug?
Or dredged from the sea? Can it be bought?
Can it be sown and harvested?
Is it a shy beast to be caught?

Death is a cloud,
immense, a clap of sound.
Love is little and not loud.
It nests within each cell, and it
cannot be split.

It is a ray, a seed, a note, a word,
a secret motion of our air and blood.
It is not alien, it is near —
our very skin —
a sheath to keep us pure of fear.

SYMMETRICAL COMPANION

It must be
there walks somewhere in the world
another
another namely like me

Not twin
but opposite
as my two hands are opposite

Where are you
my symmetrical companion?

Do you inhabit
the featureless fog
of the future?
Are you sprinting
from the shadows of the past
to overtake me?
Or are you camouflaged
in the colored present?
Do I graze you every day
as yet immune to your touch
unaware of your scent
inert under your glance?

Come to me
Whisper your name
I will know you instantly
by a passport
decipherable to ourselves alone

We shall walk uniformed
in our secret
We shall be a single reversible cloak

lined with light within
furred with dark without

Nothing shall be forbidden us
All bars shall fall before us
Even the past shall be lit behind us
and seen to have led
like two predestined corridors
to the vestibule of our meeting

We shall be two daring acrobats
above the staring faces
framed in wheels of light
visible to millions
yet revealed only to each other
in the tiny circular mirrors
of our pupils

We shall climb together
up the frail ladders
balancing on slender
but steel-strong thongs of faith
When you leap
my hands will be surely there
at the arc's limit
We shall synchronize
each step of the dance upon the wire
We shall not fall
as long as our gaze is not severed

Where are you
my symmetrical companion?

Until I find you
my mouth is locked

my heart is numb
my mind unlit
my limbs unjointed

I am a marionette
doubled up in a dark trunk
a dancer frozen
in catatonic sleep
a statue locked
in the stone
a Lazarus wrapped
in the swaddling strips
not of death
but of unborn life

a melody bound
in the strings of the viol
a torrent imprisoned
in ice
a flame buried
in the coal
a jewel hidden
in a block of lava

Come release me
Without you I do not yet exist

EVOLUTION

the stone
would like to be
Alive like me

the rooted tree
longs to be Free

the mute beast
envies my fate
Articulate

on this ball
half dark
half light
i walk Upright
i lie prone
within the night

beautiful each Shape
to see
wonderful each Thing
to name
here a stone
there a tree
here a river
there a Flame

marvelous to Stroke
the patient beasts
within their yoke

how i Yearn
for the lion
in his den
though he spurn
the touch of men

the longing
that i know
is in the Stone also
it must be

the same that rises
in the Tree
the longing
in the Lion's call
speaks for all

oh to Endure
like the stone
sufficient
to itself alone

or Reincarnate
like the tree
be born each spring
to greenery

or like the lion
without law
to roam the Wild
on velvet paw

but if walking
i meet
a Creature like me
on the street
two-legged
with human face
to recognize
is to Embrace

wonders pale
beauties dim
during my delight
with Him

an Evolution strange
two Tongues touch
exchange
a Feast unknown
to stone
or tree or beast

71

ANNUAL

(A LOVE POEM)

Beginning in the spring again
with eyes as new as leaves,
skin like the fox whose hair
hears what the river says,
nostrils locate the mole,
the turnip, the lowest stone,
tongue tastes moonlight:

beginning in the spring again,
blood wild as wind,
limbs loose as the antelope's,
and brain a basket,
lungs think air, mouth remembers
water and all transparent things:

the youngest nerve and keenest stem,
in secret shade, reach up to meet
radiance, swell to make radiance;
as all pouting blossoms do,
I turn, as earth to its sky, to you:

cave of the day's light smiling
into my throat,
meadow of stars, white
on the loam of my dream,
to your cloud-pure bones
that water my yearnings
beginning in the spring again:

turn to the lightning, your laughter
that suddens me, your hair
a wind that stings me,

your breast a fleece of birds
that hover me,
naked, dawn-colored, cool and warm,

I open to your dew,
beginning in the spring again.

To lie with you
in a field of grass
to lie there forever
and let time pass

Touching lightly
shoulder and thigh
Neither wanting more
Neither asking why

To have your whole
cool body's length
along my own
to know the strength
of a secret tide
of longing seep
into our veins
go deep . . . deep

Dissolving flesh
and melting bone
Oh to lie with you
alone

To feel your breast
rise with my sigh
To hold you mirrored
in my eye

Neither wanting more
Neither asking why

BECAUSE I DON'T KNOW

Because I don't know you, I love you:
warm cheeks, full lips, rich smile,
dark irises that slide to the side;
thick lashes, thick hair, gleaming
teeth and eyes; your hand in greeting
warmer than mine, wider, in blue shirt,
rolled sleeves, in dark jeans belted —
I liked your robust shoulders, wide neck and
tipped-up chin. That glow is blood
under skin that's warm to begin with,
almost dusky, the red showing
through — of health, of youth — but more:
your open, welcome, I-could-hug-you look.
We met once or twice, exchanged smiles:
your lips, curl-cornered to my thin,
crooked grin; your easy, laughing eyes
to my sharp stare. Did it pierce you
there, my look of hunger, like a hook?
I wanted only a sniff, a tongue-tip's
taste, a moment's bath in your rare
warmth. That last night, trading
goodbyes, when we kissed — or *you* did, me —
my hand took your nape, plunged under
the thick spill of your hair. Then
I stepped into the dark, out of the light
of the party, the screen door's yellow
square sliding smaller and smaller behind
me. You've become a dream of ripe
raspberries, in summer country: deep, dark
red lips, clean, gleaming generous smile.
Who owns you? I don't know. I'll hide you
away in my dream file. Stay there. Don't
change. I don't know you — and had better
not. Because I don't know you, I love you.

A TRELLIS FOR R.

B
L
U
E but you are R
        o
        s
        e too
and buttermilk but with blood
dots showing through.
A little salty your white

nape boy-wide. Glinting hairs shoot
back of your ears' R
         o
         s
         e that
tongue likes to feel
the maze of slip into
the funnel tell a thunder whisper to.
When I kiss

your eyes' straight lashes
down crisp go like doll's
blond straws. Glazed
iris R
    o
    s
    e
      s your lids unclose
to B
   l
   u
     e ringed targets their dark
sheen spokes almost green. I sink in
B
l
u
e black R
        o
        s
         e heart holes until
you blink.

Pink lips the serrate
folds taste smooth
and R
    o
    s
    e
    h
    i
    p round the center
bud I suck. I milknip

your two B
        l
        u
         e skeined blown R
                   o
                   s
                   e
beauties too to sniff their
berries' blood up stiff pink tips.
You're white

in patches only mostly R
                    o
                    s
                    e
buck skin and salty
speckled like a sky. I
love your spots your white neck R
                           o
                           s
                           e
your hair's wild straw splash
silk spools for your ears.
But where white spouts out spills

on your brow to clear
eyepools wheel shafts of light
R
o
s
e you are B
        l
        u
        e.

LOVE IS

a rain of diamonds
in the mind

the soul's fruit
sliced in two

a dark spring
loosed at the lips of light

under-earth waters
unlocked from their lurking
to sparkle in a crevice
parted by the sun

a temple
not of stone but cloud
beyond the heart's roar
and all violence

outside the anvil-stunned domain
unfrenzied space

between the grains of change
blue permanence

one short step
to the good ground

the bite into bread again

Dark wild honey, the lion's
eye color, you brought home
from a country store.
Tastes of the work of shaggy
bees on strong weeds,
their midsummer bloom.
My brain's electric circuit
glows, like the lion's iris
that, concentrated, vibrates
while seeming not to move.
Thick transparent amber
you brought home,
the sweet that burns.

CAT AND I

Heat of the sun on wood of the deck. Spread flat,
my body accommodates to hardness on the worn boards.
Cat fools with my foot, trying to make my big toe
stay in her ear. She gets bored when you're not here.

House feels hollow, without vibration, asleep.
No sudden bumps or door-slams, no shuffled dishes,
no water rushing in the tub, or outside from the hose.
Vacuum's snarling inhale, hedge clipper's chatter —
any welcome racket would make the little cat leap up,

land four-footed like a springbok, and race downstairs
to see what you are making happen. Instead, all is
neat and peaceful. Phone never rings. Or, if it does,
receiver waits long to be raised.

If you were here, I wouldn't be this flat, sunbathing
a whole morning on the deck, half hearing the far
gargle of a helicopter over the bay. I get lazy when
you're away. I have to feel guilty that I don't do
all the Things To Do on today's list.

Whether I ought, or not, I'm blaming it on you
that kitten doesn't spring. Slow, from inside, wags
the old Seth Thomas pendulum. And from below I hear
the suspended slaps of the tide.

Kitten has quit fooling with my toe. She's collapsed
in the shade under the overhang, her blond belly-frill
barely moving with her breath, heavy little bucket-head
dropped on paws. The crossed blue eyes are shut.

TO CONFIRM A THING

To confirm a Thing and give thanks
                 to the stars that named me
and fixed me in the Wheel of heaven
         my fate pricked out in the Boxer's chest
in the hips curled over the Horse
           Though girled in an apple-pink month
and the moon hornless
          the Brothers glitter in my wristbones
At ankle and knee I am set astride
              and made stubborn in love

In the equal Night where oracular beasts
               the planets depose
and our Selves assume their orbits
       I am flung where the Girdle's double studs
grant my destiny
              I am the Athletes in that zone
My thighs made marble-hard
          uncouple only to the Archer
with his diametrical bow
             who prances in the South
himself a part of his horse
       His gemmed arrow splits the hugging twins

The moon was gelded on that other night as well
         O his feeble kingdom we will tip over
If our feet traverse the milky way
   the earth's eccentric bead on which we balance
is small enough to hide between our toes
            its moon a mote that the Long Eye
is hardly conscious of
               nor need we be
The tough the sensuous Body our belief
          and fitting the pranks of Zeus

to this our universe
      we are Swans or Bulls as the music turns us
We are Children incorrigible and perverse
               who hold our obstinate seats
on heaven's carousel
            refusing our earth's assignment
refusing to descend
         to beget such trifles of ourselves
as the gibbous Mothers do
         We play in the Den of the Gods
and snort at death

Then let me by these signs
             maintain my magnitude
as the candid Centaur his dynasty upholds
          And in the Ecliptic Year
our sweet rebellions
        shall not be occulted but remain
coronals in heaven's Wheel

On the Cliff

I'm sawing a slice off that hard dark knobby loaf
from Zabar's — black molasses and raisins in it —
to have with Tilsit cheese. You left a pumpkin and
autumn leaves on the stripped wood table, you filled
the birdfeeder hanging from the eaves. The window
is clean, the sill is varnished, white impatiens
in a brick clay pot smile above the sink. Our terrace
lined with boulders, the slate path with pachysandra
you planted. Storm doors are on, in front and back,
it's snug in here. I'm chewing, looking at the shelves
you cut and hung to hold our books and decoys.
You're strong, you twist off the lids of jars.
Cold nights you're a stove in bed.

By the Canal

For Valentine's Day a whole studio and library!
Shelves built to the ceiling, there's space for every
thing: papers, folders, files and books, books, books.
Binoculars and chess set, tape recorders, tapes and
jigsaw. Telephone that's a blue car has a shelf
of its own. The old maple sawhorse table fits right in
and looks brand new. Curly ivy on the sill and outside
an entire alphabet of birds, on the porch, in the yard.
You put pink ribbons of sunrise in the back window,
scarlet bands of sunset in the front, the moon above our
bed at night. It snowed. You made a path. The Christmas
poinsettia blooms all year.

EQUILIBRIST

I'm coming toward you
always
instep on the quivering wire
leaning aside
but never looking down
eyes unsmiling
immune to sleep
or hazard

I'm coming toward you

Always your pallid image leaps
behind the bars of distance
where merge sea and sky

Not setting with the sun
nor waning with the moon
your torso centaur-like
is prancing
upon my mind's rim

Fiercely taking aim
my body is a sharpened dart
of longing
coming toward you always

ABOUT THE POET

May Swenson was born May 28, 1913, in Logan, Utah, and died December 4, 1989, in Ocean View, Delaware. In that lifetime she worked as a newspaper reporter, secretary, ghost writer, editor, poet-in-residence, but always and mainly as a poet, publishing 450 poems of the 800 she wrote. All of these are love letters to the world, for she loved life and rejoiced in celebrating it. Her poems appeared in *Antaeus, The Atlantic Monthly, Carleton Miscel-lany, The Nation, The New Yorker, Paris Review, Parnassus, Poetry,* and in eleven published volumes. These earned for her much praise from fellow poets, a place in the hearts and minds of poetry lovers, and many awards, among them the Brandeis University Creative Arts Award, Rockefeller, Guggenheim, and Ford fellowships, the Bollingen Prize for Poetry, a grant from the National Endowment for the Arts, an honorary doctor of letters degree from Utah State University, and a MacArthur Fellowship. She was a member of the American Academy and Institute of Arts and Letters and a chancellor of the Academy of American Poets.